Close Encounters with Jesus

Close Encounters with Jesus

Bill Nichols

Close Encounters with Jesus

© Bill Nichols 2018

This book is a work of fiction. Named locations are used fictitiously, and characters and incidents are the product of the author's imagination. Any resemblance to actual events or places or persons, living or dead, is entirely coincidental.

All rights reserved. Without limiting the rights under copyright reserved above, no part of this publication may be reproduced, stored in a retrieval system, or transmitted, in any form or by any means (electronic, mechanical, photocopying, recording or otherwise), without the prior written permission of the copyright owner of this book.

Published by
Lighthouse Christian Publishing
SAN 257-4330
5531 Dufferin Drive
Savage, Minnesota, 55378
United States of America

www.lighthousechristianpublishing.com

Bill Nichols

The Adulterous Woman

It was a bad way to start out a day. She had fulfilled a commitment that should not have been made in the first place. It had always been safe for them, but not today. Somehow someone had caught on to them. They were followed this time. The men had waited for a while and then came right in and caught them in the act. Some man threw a robe around her and off they went. Where they were headed, she didn't know.

Down the street they took her. The people in the shops and booths stared as the religious leaders hustled her along with them. As they went, there were more of the religious types joining them. It was as if this had all been finely planned. They seemed to be headed toward the Temple. She had not been to that part of town for a long time. They busted through the gate. As they entered, they slowed some. There, a short way off, was a simple-looking man seated in front of a crowd. They seemed to be listening to him. He seemed to be teaching them.

The men shoved her in front of the man. She tripped and fell at his feet. She tried her best to stay covered by the robe. The leader of the group of men spoke to the man teaching a crowd of people. This leader explained to the man that this woman had been caught right in the middle of the act of adultery. He explained that the Law of Moses said that she should be stoned to death. Then he asked the man what he thought should be done.

The man who had been teaching stood up in the middle of the men. He looked around as if something or someone was missing in the group. The woman kept her head down and her eyes to the ground. Somehow her life seemed to be in the hands of this stranger. Much to her surprise, the man did not immediately answer the religious leaders. He bent down right in front of her and began to write in the dirt. She could not tell what he wrote. He was facing her and the words were upside down for her. The other men seem agitated that he was writing in the dirt. They seemed to think he was ignoring them or didn't hear the question. They kept repeating the question. They got louder and louder.

Suddenly the man who had been writing in the dirt stood up and looked at the religious leaders, one at a time. The teaching man very calmly, but with a definite sense of authority, spoke to the men. He said, "If anyone of you is without sin, let him be the first to throw a stone at her." After he had said this he again knelt in front of the woman and wrote in the dirt.

It was quiet. The woman braced herself for the first rock. Her muscles tensed. She heard a thump. The sound made her jump. Then she realized that there was no pain; no blood. Then there were more thumps. With her head still down she lifted her eyes just enough to see rocks hitting the ground and feet moving away from her. Finally there was silence. She could see the teaching man still writing on the ground. She could see the crowd he had been teaching out of the corner of her eye. They all sat still.

The teaching man stood up and helped her stand. He looked into her eyes and said, "Woman, where are they? Has no one condemned you?" She was able to look at what was left. All that was there was the listening crowd, the teaching man and her. There on the ground were all the rocks left by the religious men. She answered him, "No one, sir." He just stood there in front of her a moment. The look on his face was so peaceful! The teaching man said one more thing to her, "Then neither do I condemn you. Go now and leave your life of sin."

She was not sure what to do for a moment. The man looked down at the ground. He took his foot and rubbed out the things he had written on the ground. He looked back up at her and nodded. She wrapped herself as well as she could. She had to go back down through town again. She had to get her life back together. As she walked, she wondered who that teaching man was. She had never met anyone like him.

The Adulterous Woman (In Depth)

The story of Jesus meeting the adulterous woman can only be found in the Gospel of John. Some Bibles list this account as, "Jesus forgives an adulterous woman."

With a close reading of this story we may find these titles do not exactly describe what Jesus did on that day. To help with this study it will be necessary for us to back up in the Scriptures to get a complete picture of this story.

In John 7:32-52, the Pharisees devised a plan to capture and get rid of Jesus. He was beginning to be a problem, interfering with their attempts to keep things the way they wanted. The acts of miracles done by Jesus and the things he said had stirred the people. "People were saying, 'When the Christ comes, will he do more miraculous signs than this man'?" (John 7:31) The speaking of the words "Jesus" and "the Christ" in the same sentence did not cause enthusiasm in the Pharisees. When the Pharisees heard about these comments, "The chief priests and the Pharisees sent temple guards to arrest Jesus." (John 7:32)

The result of this action did not turn out the way the Pharisees had intended. The temple guards listened to Jesus as he taught the people. "Finally the temple guards went back to the chief priests and Pharisees, who asked them, 'Why didn't you bring him in?' 'No one ever spoke the way this man does,' the guards declared." (John 7:45-46)

Now we have the atmosphere for the story found in John 8:1-11. Because of the animosity of the religious leaders in Jerusalem, Jesus went to the Mount of Olives. It was there he spent long hours in prayer. Jesus' practice was to separate himself from the crowds to pray and renew his mission and spirit. We know by the Scriptures (John 8:2) that at dawn Jesus appeared in the temple courts again. He was there to teach the people about the kingdom of God. As he taught, the people would come in large numbers to hear him. The religious leaders were having a difficult time with Jesus and what he said, and his presence in the temple courts would only complicate the situation. By now the Jewish religious leaders would do almost anything to trap Jesus and arrest him.

The religious leaders, knowing Jesus was here in the temple courts, took this opportunity to try to trap him. John 8:3 tells us it was the teachers of the law who brought forth the "woman caught in adultery." The Jewish leaders had chosen to send their best to confront and attempt to trap Jesus. They must have thought this carpenter from Nazareth would be no match for their professors of religious law. But they were wrong.

The scene as we understand it was one that involved enough of a crowd to make this event a public spectacle. The Pharisees chose this time because of the number of people listening to Jesus teach. They would embarrass him in front of those who had come to respect him. As Jesus was teaching he was approached by these experts in the Law of Moses. They brought with them a woman who was reportedly caught in the act of adultery. The men with her began by telling Jesus about this woman and her crime, "Teacher, this woman was caught in the act of adultery." (John 8:4)

The Pharisees did know their law. What they said was true. They took their law from the first five books of the Old Testament. In Leviticus 20:10 we are told, "If a man commits adultery with another man's wife — with the wife of his neighbor — both the adulterer and the adulteress must be put to death." In Deuteronomy 22:22 it says, "If a man is found sleeping with another man's wife, both the man who slept with her and the woman must die. You must purge the evil from Israel."

The Pharisees attempted to obey the law found in Deuteronomy 22:22 by executing the woman. But we should ask these Pharisees "Where was the man?" The law is clear that both parties should receive the same punishment. If the woman had been caught in the act of adultery, someone else must have been involved. But that other person does not appear in this story. This requires us to look at the motive of the Pharisees. Some think that the Pharisees knew Jesus would be in the Temple teaching that morning, and held the woman overnight in order to use her in this plot.

The Pharisees sought to put Jesus squarely between the Law of Moses and the Roman law. If Jesus said that the woman should not be punished by death and should be let go, he would be going against the Law of Moses. If he said she should be put to death according to the Law of Moses, the Pharisees would have immediately taken him to the Roman authorities for condemning a person to death, which was against the Roman law for any Jew. The Pharisees thought they had set the perfect trap for this uneducated carpenter.

Much to the surprise of the Pharisees that day, Jesus did not say anything in response to the question. John's Gospel tells us Jesus bent down and started to write on the ground with his finger. There is no indication what he wrote. Since the Gospel does not tell us, we shall honor the silence on that point and not speculate. While Jesus wrote on the ground, the Pharisees seemed confused about what he was doing there. They kept on questioning him. Instead of answering the question, Jesus put the resolution of this situation back on the condemners. He said, "If anyone of you is without sin, let him be the first to throw a stone at her." And again he stooped down and wrote more on the ground. Here before Jesus was an embarrassed, condemned woman and the Jewish elite, who considered themselves as the set apart, the righteous ones. Now, the righteous ones had to deal with his question. John tells us that the accusers went away one at a time.

The final scene consists only of Jesus and the woman — and, we must not forget, those who came to hear Jesus teach that day. They had been witnesses of this entire exchange. Jesus taught a great lesson right in front of them. He was not finished. We can only imagine the body language between Jesus and the Pharisees, and then between Jesus and the woman. With the woman standing there, Jesus straightened up and asked her, "Woman, where are they? Has no one condemned you?" She answers, "No one, sir." She does not know who this man is. Jesus responds, "Then neither do I condemn you. Go now and leave your life of sin." There are no words of forgiveness spoken here. Neither are there words of condemnation. Jesus calmly and with authority instructs the woman to end her life of sin.

The story ends there. We do not know what the woman did next. We can only imagine what changes must have taken place in her life. The woman is not mentioned again. We never knew her name. She will be forever known as the woman caught in adultery. That was how she was known to the crowd listening to Jesus teaching that day. We can only hope the rest of her story was a witness to the saving, changing grace of God through Jesus Christ, his only Son.

Questions

How is the nature of God shown in this story?

How do you see the nature of man in this story?

How were the Pharisees using the Law of Moses in the story?

Are there people using the rules of the law in the same way today?

Did Jesus actually forgive the woman?

Do you perceive what he said as condoning what she did?

In what ways would the woman have to change to leave her life of sin?

What was the lesson for the crowd that day?

Barabbas

In the Gospels there is a person mentioned named Barabbas. The character and person of Barabbas is not all that clear. What we know about Barabbas is given to us in the four Gospels. The facts are that Barabbas was in prison for taking parting in a rebellion against the Romans and for murder. Some think he was a thief. There is a hint that he was well known to the crowd at Pilate's palace. Some in Judea may have thought of Barabbas as some as sort of a national hero for his role in the rebellion.

The facts about the who and what of Barabbas fade some as his role on that Good Friday pushes him into the story of day of Jesus' crucifixion. Pilate annually released one prisoner during the Passover Feast. This day he offered the release of either Barabbas the murderer, or of Jesus, some called the king of the Jews. He did not line up all the prisoners and say, "Pick one." The Gospels tell us Pilate only offered these two. For the crowd, it was a more a matter of condemning Jesus to death than choosing to release Barabbas. The chief priests and elders wanted to be rid of Jesus any way they could and this gave them a way to do it. That's what we know from the Gospels.

Let's do some wondering beyond the Gospels, going beyond the stories told by Matthew, Mark, Luke and John. We can imagine the people involved: Jesus, Pilate, the chief priests and the crowd. The person in this story that is not clear to us is Barabbas. How would Barabbas see this entire scene? What might be going through his mind as this unfolds?

There is no evidence that Barabbas witnessed this event. But what if he did? We might find Barabbas stuck away in some dark and dirty dungeon that everyone knew was death row for Roman prisoners in Jerusalem. We find him suddenly stirred by the sound of the soldiers coming his way. He could hear the noise outside and knew something important was about to happen. Maybe his mind raced to the conclusion: "This is it! Today is my day to die." Then the soldiers took him out of his cell.

The Roman troops led Barabbas up through Pilate's palace. He saw more and more light. That much light began to hurt his eyes. He had not seen sunlight for weeks. The sound of a crowd grew louder and louder. At last Barabbas was led outside the palace. He saw Pilate seated on the judgment seat. He knew that was not a good sign for him. Then the sight of that huge crowd caught his eye. He knew many of the people in that large group. Those were people who watched him grow up in that city. Sprinkled among the crowd were the Jewish leaders. Barabbas wondered if they had come to see him condemned and crucified. His eyes came to rest on a lone figure standing on the other side of Pilate. As he looked at this man he wondered who he was. The man was dressed in a purple robe, and on his head was a crude crown made out of thorns. What surprised Barabbas was that the man seemed at total peace with what is happening in that place.

As Barabbas stood before the crowd, he remembered that Pilate would release one prisoner every year at this time. His hopes of being set free rose, but were tempered as he looked at the other man. There was something different about that man, but Barabbas can't quite decide what that difference was. Pilate stood and announced that he would set one of the prisoners free. "Will it be Barabbas or Jesus, called the Christ?" he asked. Now Barabbas wondered what kind of man would claim he was the Messiah. Then the crowd began to speak in one voice. They called his name — "Barabbas! Barabbas!" He was the one they wanted released on this day. He couldn't believe what he was hearing! When Pilate asked the question a second time the crowd called "Barabbas" even louder. Barabbas looked over at the other man, who still seemed at peace, almost as if he had known the outcome before this ordeal started. For the first time, Barabbas thought, "It should be me, not him." Pilate gave in to the crowd. He ordered Barabbas to be released and for this man, Jesus, to be flogged. The soldiers took the chains off Barabbas and told him he was free to go.

At first Barabbas just stood there. What had just happened did not seem real to him. Then he began to walk down the steps of the palace. He was a bit fearful that this trial could fall apart for him and that he would have to go back to prison. Then realized that no one was paying attention to him at all. Their attention was fixed on what was happening to this man, Jesus.

Barabbas tried to leave as fast he could. He did not think it was safe to stay near that crowd very long. But as he started to walk away the crowd began to move toward this other man, now held by the soldiers. The soldiers stripped the clothes from his back and began flogging him. It was a horrible sight. The sound of each whack caused Barabbas to flinch. He could not seem to move. He could not keep from watching this man being flogged. For a second time he thought, "That should be me, not him."

After they finished flogging the man, the soldiers brought out a cross. They put the cross on the man's back and led him out to be crucified. Rather than escaping into the safety of the city of Jerusalem, Barabbas chose to become part of the crowd following this man Jesus as he carried his cross toward his death. The crowd was full of curious people and others who were delighted that this man was finally going to be stopped from his interference with their religion. Barabbas stayed on the fringes of the crowd, still concerned that things could change for him. He had already been forgotten and he was glad for that. The attention of the crowd was on this man as he carried his cross through the city. As he walked Jesus fell under the weight of the cross and the soldiers ordered another man to carry his cross. Barabbas was surprised to find a lump in his throat and a tear running down his cheek. He was feeling sympathy for this man who was about to die! Again he found the thought came to his mind, "That should be me, not him."

Some of the crowd followed Jesus as he headed out to the place of crucifixion. There were people along the road watching the man struggle to walk. Barabbas stood watching that group as they headed up the hill to the place of death. He was compelled to go up there with them. He arrived at the top of the hill just as the soldiers were nailing Jesus to the cross. Each time he heard the hammer hit the nail Barabbas cringed. This time the thought came faster, "That should be me, not him." The soldiers leaned the cross forward and Barabbas heard it make a "thunk" sound as it went into its hole.

Then he stood still, watching the man on the cross. He heard him as he spoke. He was amazed as the man forgave those who were executing him! He heard and saw him speak to his mother. He heard him as he spoke to one of the thieves on another cross. Barabbas kept standing there watching what was happening that day. He stood for a long time. At one point Barabbas was sure Jesus was looking at him. He was afraid to look at that man on the cross, but he could not. Barabbas found a place in the shadows where he could watch. He sat down. As he sat he put his face in his hands and cried. It had been a long time since he had cried. What he saw happen had reached his heart and soul.

Then he watched as the man died. A soldier stuck a spear into his side to make sure Jesus was dead. Barabbas could not stop the thought coming one more time, "That should be me, not him." It was then that Barabbas realized that this man Jesus had died in his place. He had given his life for Barabbas' life; it was freedom from death. He waited for a while. Two men came and took Jesus down from the cross. He heard them say they were going to bury him. With that assurance Barabbas headed back down that hill and back into Jerusalem. As he walked he decided he wanted to find out more about this man Jesus. He would seek some of Jesus' followers so he could find out who he was. He began to feel a strange sense of peace come over him as he thought about that. That is what he would do. He had to know about this man who had given his life in exchange for his.

Barabbas

(In Depth)

A study of the story of Barabbas includes many other people, as far as the Gospels are concerned; he is but a small player in the story of Jesus' life. The first group we encounter in this Good Friday story are the chief priest and elders. The chief priest was named Caiaphas. Caiaphas was his surname; his given name is Joseph. He was appointed chief priest in 18 A.D. He ruled in that position from 18-37 A.D. He is mostly known for his role in Jesus' trial. As you read the story of the trials of Jesus you will notice that the term "high priests" is often used. That indicates more than one high priest. The other high priest was Annas. He was high priest from 6-15 AD. John 18:12-24 describes Jesus being questioned by Annas. Many of the Jews saw the role of high priest as one that lasted a lifetime. So even though Caiaphas had been appointed as the high priest, Annas was revered as a high priest. In modern day language he might be thought of as the High Priest emeritus.

The next person in this story is Pontius Pilate. Several times in the Gospel account he is referred to as the governor. He was the fifth procurator of Judea (26-36 AD.) His rule included the time of ministry of John the Baptist and Jesus of Nazareth. Some think of Pilate as a worldly man who seemed anxious to do the right thing but had no desire to take a risk that might involve personal sacrifice. His job would have included keeping the peace in Judea by whatever means necessary. He would have had to make sure that the taxes were kept up so that the needs of the Roman Empire would be met, even that far from Rome. He would have some control of the troops stationed there. In case of some kind of unrest or rebellion he would have instructed the troops to use their strength to suppress it.

The Gospel indicates that Pilate had to deal with two unexpected forces on the day of Jesus' trial. The first group was the chief priests and elders, later joined by the crowd. They wanted him to execute Jesus. The other force was his wife. Her name seems to have been Abrokla. She could have been a Jewish woman who married Pilate. She could have been favorable to Jesus and his ministry. She had a dream about Jesus and the trial the night before the event of his crucifixion. Her suggestion to Pilate was, "to have nothing to do with this man."

There is agreement among the Gospels that it was Pilate's custom in his role as governor to release one prisoner during the Passover Feast. Because he eventually gave in to the wishes of the chief priests, elders and the crowd, some consider him weak. There is a way of viewing this that says Pilate was working past his level of understanding and control. Some evidence of his state of mind comes to us in John 19:10 when Pilate says to Jesus, "Do you refuse to speak to me? Don't you realize I have power either to free you or to crucify you?"

Pilate will always be remembered for his role in Jesus' death that day. Whether out of strength or weakness he had a role in the death of Christ. One odd part of his story is sometimes forgotten. It comes in Matthew 27:24: "When Pilate saw he was getting nowhere, but instead uproar was starting, he took water and washed his hands in front of the crowd. 'I am innocent of this man's blood,' he said. 'It is your responsibility'." Pilate may have facilitated the crucifixion of Jesus in order to be politically correct in Judea on a certain Friday that we know as Good Friday.

The crowd was a large part of the story of this Good Friday. It was made up of small, interconnected groups. One of the groups in the crowd was that of the chief priests and elders. In Luke 23:13 we are told that Pilate called together the chief priests, the rulers and the people. The use of the terms "elders" and "rulers" is not well defined. A clue to which they were is found in Mark 15:1, "Very early in the morning, the chief priests, with the elders, the teachers of the law and the whole Sanhedrin, reached a decision. They bound Jesus, led him away and handed him over to Pilate." If they were part of the crowd, then we would most likely find Jesus' friend Nicodemus in that group. We might also have found Joseph of Arimathea, who later buried Jesus in his new tomb.

Finally we find that group in the crowd simply known as "the people." One scholar suggests the chief priests commanded their servants to be a part of this event. Whoever they were, they were there that day and helped condemn Jesus to death.

When it came time to choose between Barabbas and Jesus, called the Christ, we are told they were together in their choice. "They shouted." "With one voice they cried out." The crowd had a choice of which prisoner would be freed that day. They said, "Give us Barabbas." When asked what should be done with Jesus, they shouted, "Crucify him." There is an odd interaction between Pilate and the crowd. Remember that Pilate washed his hands and said, "I am innocent of this man's blood. It is your responsibility." The crowd gave this strange response, "All the people answered, 'Let his blood be on us and our children'." The crowd made a choice and would live with the consequences of their rejection of God's son.

Now we move to Jesus in this story. This is really his story. It is a story that lifts him up as the Son of God and Savior of the world. In his final night and day he endured what he had told his disciples, "We are going up to Jerusalem, and the Son of Man will be betrayed to the chief priests and teachers of the law. They will condemn him to death and will turn him over to the Gentiles to be mocked and flogged and crucified. On the third day he will be raised to life!" (Matthew 20:17-19) With his followers scattered, one who betrayed him and one who denied him, Jesus had to go through this terrible day alone. He endured the many trials. He endured the hatred of the chief priests, elders and the crowd. He endured the mocking by the soldiers. He endured the pain of the nails and the crucifixion. He finally died. He died knowing he was not defeated. When he spoke the words, "It is finished," he knew that part of his mission was complete.

Finally, we come to the person of Barabbas, the focus of this study. Even though he was but a bit player in the story of Jesus his role was important. The high priests wanted to destroy Jesus. They seemed to have little interest in setting this murderer free. But he was handy in the scheme of things that day. They had two options, Barabbas or Jesus, but there was no way they could allow Jesus to go free. That sealed his fate and put Barabbas in the strange place of being the one chosen to have freedom.

The four Gospels give us little information about this man, Barabbas. Matthew calls him a "notorious prisoner." Mark and Luke indicate he "was in prison with insurrectionists for murder." He was the one chosen from the group of insurrectionists to be an option for release against Jesus on that day. Speculation might cause us to think Pilate picked the worst of the prisoners to Jesus' (called the Christ) "other option." Pilate may have been very surprised that Barabbas was the one chosen for release.

Barabbas' name leaves room for some different opinions on its meaning. Some scholars think his name means, "The son of a man." The thought is that he was the spoiled child of a doting father. Another thought is that he was considered truly the son of the devil. We do not know if he had a father whom locals thought of as the devil, or if because of his ruthlessness he was seen as the devil's son. Another group of scholars lean toward his name meaning, "the son of a master." That leaves us wondering what kind of master that might be. The last definition moves us to a deeper consideration about who he might have been. A final possibility about the meaning of his name is that it indicates that he was the son of a rabbi. Could it be that Barabbas was the son of the Jewish equivalent of a preacher? That would mean Jesus died in the place of a preacher's son on that Good Friday.

With our focus on Barabbas in this study, we can agree that he was no model citizen. What we know about him from the Gospels is that on a certain day in Jerusalem he found himself as one of the two prisoners with the possibility to be set free by the crowd at Pilate's palace. Instead of Jesus, called the Christ, Barabbas was chosen by the crowd and released. We do not know any more.

We can only hope that Barabbas came to realize that Jesus had given his life for his. Then we can hope that this knowledge changed his life.

Questions

Where do you find the nature of God in action in the story of Barabbas?

In what ways do you see the nature of man at work in the story?

Have you ever considered that Jesus died in your place as he did for Barabbas?

Have you ever felt like you washed your hands of Jesus like Pilate did?

In thinking of Barabbas, do you think there might be some people who are beyond the salvation Jesus offers from the cross?

Have you ever found yourself going along with the crowd?

Healing the Blind Men
Bartimaeus

This day started out like every other day. He rose from his little, shabby shelter. He felt around for the bread he had saved. Someone had given him some bread the day before, probably out of pity. He did not know who it was. It must have been a stranger headed for Jerusalem. The traffic on the road had increased in the past few days. People were making their way to Jerusalem. The Feast of the Passover was about to start. The crowds would only get bigger. He would not be going to the celebration of the Feast. He was blind and was not welcome at the Temple. He was considered unclean and was not able to sacrifice to the Lord.

He continued his morning routine. The roosters had done their job of waking him. He readied himself as good as he could. He surrounded himself with his cloak and headed off for his spot by the side of the road. Years ago he had found a favorable place outside Jericho on the road to Jerusalem. There at that spot he waited all day every day for hand outs from people who took pity on him, the blind man named Bartimaeus.

The days were getting warmer. The warmth and the coming of the Passover celebration seemed to make people happier to give something to a blind beggar on the side of the road. He knew he had competition. There was a blind man who sat on the roadside on the other side of town. He must have thought the pickings were better on the way in to town. There was another blind man who sat closer to the center of town. Then there was Bartimaeus. He was right at the edge of Jericho. He thought it best to be the last opportunity to be charitable to a blind man before reaching the outskirts of Jerusalem. There were plenty of beggars there.

As the morning wore on he could hear people talking about a blind man who had been healed that morning. He sat quietly so he could find out the details. As he listened he realized the blind man who had been healed was the man who regularly stationed himself on the way in to Jericho. Bartimaeus couldn't quite believe what he had heard. He thought, "If he could be healed maybe I can be healed."

Bartimaeus could hear a lot of noise from the center of town. The sounds were different than those of a usual day. He could hear that there was a large crowd back in town and could not tell why. He did what he always did. He sat, waited and listened. As people passed by he could hear them speaking of a man named Jesus of Nazareth. Bartimaeus had heard that name. Each time the discussion had been about the wonderful things this man had done.

Maybe this Jesus was in Jericho. Maybe he was the one who had healed the blind man on the other side of town. For the first time in a long time Bartimaeus felt some hope in his life.

As the sun moved and warmed him he could hear the conversations change as people passed by him. At one time some people stopped to drop some coins his way. They stood near him and talked about the stranger who had gone to visit Zacchaeus. The people were upset that a so-called prophet and teacher would lower himself to spend time with such a thief. Bartimaeus knew the name, Zacchaeus. He was the local chief of tax collectors and had a terrible reputation. The people of Jericho hated Zacchaeus. He had become a rich man at the expense of the people of the area. Zacchaeus meant little to Bartimaeus for he had nothing to tax. He was interested in what they said about this Jesus. He kept up his hope that maybe this man would pass his way. He would sit, wait and hope that he might meet Jesus.

The activity back in Jericho signaled to him that the normal afternoon activity had come. He could tell people had finished their mid-day meal. Life would slow down for a while. The traffic in his part of the road was usually less about this time of the day. Sometimes people would give him something left over after their meal. There came a stir from the center of town. Bartimaeus could not make out what was causing such a crowd at this time of day. He could tell it was a good sized crowd headed his way. He could tell there were some men standing in front of him. They seemed to be looking back into town. They began talking about the man called Jesus.

Bartimaeus could not stand it any longer. He had to find out what was happening. He shouted to the men, "What is it? What's happening?" One of the men answered him, "It's Jesus of Nazareth. He's headed this way. He healed a blind man this morning, has spent some of the day with that scoundrel Zacchaeus and is headed this way. That is what you hear. It is all his followers and him headed to Jerusalem." The sounds grew louder and louder. They were almost upon him. This was his chance. He took it. As he sat by the side of the road, he lifted his hands and shouted, "Jesus, Son of David have mercy on me." Some of the men at the front of the crowd tried to get him to be quiet. He would not be silenced. He shouted again, even louder than before, "Son of David, have mercy on me."

By the sound of feet he could tell the crowd had stopped. He could hear a man say something, but he was too far away to be sure what it was. Just then some men grabbed him by the arms and began moving him toward that voice. They said, "Cheer up! On your feet! He's calling you." Bartimaeus wondered if this could be a miracle day for him?

The men leading him stopped. He could hear people all around him. He heard a voice, "What do you want for me to do for you?" He said, "Rabbi, I want to see." The man said back to him, "Go, your faith has healed you." As soon as those words hit his ears Bartimaeus could see. It was the first time in his life he could see what was around him. The brightness of the sun made him shield his eyes. He put up his hand and looked for the face that went with that voice. He knew who it was when a man reached out and put his hand on Bartimaeus' shoulder. There was a smile on the man's face. It was the first smile he had ever seen. Then Jesus just walked off toward Jerusalem with the people following him. The crowd with Jesus parted around Bartimaeus as the left, all except one. The man just grinned at him. He said, "Aren't you Bartimaeus?" In response Bartimaeus nodded. The man said, "My name is Samuel. I was the blind beggar who sat by the road on the other side of town. That was until this morning. Jesus healed me too. I went with him to the house of Zacchaeus. That was the best food I have ever eaten." Bartimaeus asked, "What do we do now?" Samuel answered, "We follow him." He pointed toward Jesus and the group that followed him on the road. Bartimaeus gathered up his cloak and the donations for the day. Then Samuel and he headed down the road to catch up with Jesus on his way to Jerusalem.

Healing the Blind Men
(In Depth)

Read Mark 10:46-52

Additional reading can be found in Matthew 20:29-34 and Luke 18:35-43

If you grew up reading and hearing about the healing of Blind Bartimaeus you may a bit surprised with the entire story of that day. As one man used to say, "Stay tune for the rest of the story." As we do any Bible study we need to put the story we are reading into context. We will be helped if we know where it fits in the ministry and life of Jesus.

The story of Jesus healing the blind men comes as he is making his way to Jerusalem for the final time. Matthew, Mark and Luke all place this story as Jesus nears the city. In Matthew 20:17-19 we are told, "Now as Jesus was going up to Jerusalem, he took the twelve disciples aside and said to them, "We are going up to Jerusalem, and the Son of Man will be betrayed to the chief priests and teachers of the law. They will condemn him to death and turn him over to the Gentiles to be mocked and flogged and crucified. On the third day he will be raised to life!" This was the third time Jesus had predicted his own death. He could have not gotten any plainer about the future than that. Another thing of note about the placement of this story is that it is just before Jesus rides into Jerusalem on a donkey in Matthew and Mark. In Luke there is the story of Jesus' meeting with Zacchaeus and a parable then Jesus rides into Jerusalem in his Triumphal Entry.

As we study the story we find in Matthew, Mark and Luke we may find that we do not have one story of a man or two blind men being healed. We may, in fact, have different stories that involve the healing of three separate men. The three stories all happened at the town of Jericho, which was about ten miles from Jerusalem. Jesus was headed for Jerusalem where he would suffer many things, be crucified and be raised again on the third day. As he traveled toward Jericho the Scriptures indicate that he passed by a blind man as he was approaching the town. (Luke 18:35) Then we are told in Mark 10:46 that as "they came to Jericho" Jesus is stopped by a blind man, named Bartimaeus. We are also told that as Jesus was leaving Jericho," he is stopped by two blind men. Are these three accounts the same story or different ones? Or could they be related in some way?

In John Gill's Exposition of the Bible, he indicated that even though Matthew mentions two men, Mark only a blind man named, Bartimaeus and Luke speaks only of a blind man that it is quite possible that this story is three in one. Where we read the Gospel account we find that on the same day in the same town three blind were healed and received their sight. The accounts of the stories are so close in what happens and what is said. All of the men shout similar phrases when they discover who is passing by them. They all shout either "Jesus" or "Lord." Then they are reported to say, "Have mercy on me!" Or "Have mercy on us!" At this point of each story some in the crowd tries to make each of the men be quiet. We cannot tell for sure if these people are friends or foes of Jesus. If they are friends that are trying to quiet the men, it could be because they knew Jesus was being hunted by the Jewish religious leaders. If they are foes they may be offended at the terms the men are using, "Son of David." That was the well known phrase for the One who was the Messiah. The reaction of the men to those who would quiet them was to shout more and probably louder. Again, each of them spoke the name, "Son of David," as they called to Jesus.

These men seemed to be no strangers to the reputation of Jesus and the works of miracles he had already done. He had healed the blind before he came to Jericho. (Matthew 9:27-31) Even though they were blind they man have heard about the work of the Promised One:

> "Then will the eyes of the blind be opened
> and the ears of the deaf unstopped.
> Then will the lame leap like a deer,
> and the mute tongue will shout for joy."
> *Isaiah 35:5*

The stories go on to tell us Jesus' reaction to these blind men. In each account we are told that Jesus stopped when he heard these men. Keep in mind that Jesus had his face and mind set on Jerusalem and what he had to do there. He then had each man brought to him. Jesus asked the same question in all three accounts, "What do you want me to do for you?" These men could have asked for anything. Jesus may have remembered those who followed him only because he could multiply bread and fish. Although the three accounts vary in what name they called Jesus, they asked for the same thing, "I want to see," or "We want our sight." They did not hedge about what they wanted. They came out straight forward and asked for the healing of what they knew as the one thing that held them back in life.

Jesus' response for these men was to have great compassion for them. Matthew reports he touched the eyes of the two men. Mark says Jesus spoke to Bartimaeus saying, "Go, your faith has healed you." Luke tells us that Jesus spoke to the man, "Receive your sight, your faith has healed you." Some times we get nervous about the faith and healing issue. "Could it be that I would be healed if I just had enough faith?" The faith of these men was the channel through which healing could occur. Their belief and trust that Jesus could do this thing allowed the work of Jesus to complete the wholeness in these men. The faith they had was enough for Jesus. All the men were immediately healed. All followed Jesus. Couldn't it be possible that the blind man Jesus healed on the way in to Jericho was able to witness the healing of Bartimaeus and the other man? Can you imagine his joy? If they did follow Jesus could they have been part of the crowd who welcomed Jesus as he rode into Jerusalem on a donkey?

Let's back up some and look at these men in these stories. All of the Gospels agree that the men were blind and sitting by the roadside. Mark and Luke tell us that Bartimaeus and a blind man were there begging as they sat by the road. For most who have studied this story the focus has been on Bartimaeus. It seems that he was the more well known of the three men. There is some particular interest about the name Bartimaeus that calls for our attention. A study of the name in The Strongest NIV Exhaustive Concordance tells us "Bartimaeus" means "son of Tamai or Son of uncleanness." Maybe Bartimaeus was well known for this father's lack of hygiene. From John Gill's Exposition of the Bible we find an alternate view of the name. Gill thinks the name Tima or Timaeus moves us toward the name Ben Tima or the Son of Tima or Timaeus. Origen thought the name related more to Time in our language rather than uncleanness. The name spoke of honor. Bartimaeus' father many have been an honorable and successful man in Jericho.

We find these blind men in a sad state. Each morning these blind men must make their way to what they considered the best spot along the road to beg. Their sightless condition kept them from functioning as useful citizens in their home town. When Jesus healed these three men he healed their lives at several levels. The healing brought wholeness to them. First they were healed physically. When they came to Jesus they could not see. When Jesus spoke and touched them they could immediately see. Whether they had been born blind or not did not matter at this point. Now they could see the world around them. Secondly Jesus healed the spiritual eyes of these men. They had called him, "Lord." They had recognized him as, "Son of David," which is a sign they thought he was the Messiah. They displayed faith and confidence in the man, Jesus. Finally, these healings restored the place of these men in their community, families and faith group. They could now join in work that was meaningful. They no longer had to sit by the roadside and beg. Their families had no need to look at them in shame. Their blindness connected them to sin either for their family or themselves in that time. They were no longer seen as unclean so they could go to the Temple to worship. When Jesus healed them he healed all there was about them.

There is one final thing we must examine. Jesus asked each of the men, "What do you want me to do?" He still asks us that question.

Questions

How do you see the nature of God at work in the story of Bartimaeus?

In what ways do you see the nature of man in the story?

How do you think Bartimaeus' life would change after he was healed?

Why do you think those around Jesus tried to keep Bartimaeus from Jesus?

If Jesus asked you, "What do you want me to do for you?" what would your answer be?

Nicodemus

Nicodemus had spent a lifetime reading the Scriptures. Even though he was an expert in the Law of Moses, he read the other parts, too. He had read about the promises of God. The one that interested him the most was the promise of a coming Messiah. He was a keen observer of how people kept the law. It was his job. The law seemed to be more and more oppressive. It was supposed to bring fullness to life. Even for those who proclaimed themselves righteous, the law had become a heavy load. Nicodemus was now in search of mercy to come in the form of the Messiah.

Lately, Nicodemus had become interested in a man name John, the one called The Baptizer. This man was a bit strange. He wore odd clothes and was said to eat honey and locusts. But this John fellow was saying some things that drew great crowds. He was preaching about repentance. He was saying, "Repent for the kingdom of heaven is near." That message seemed to be one people wanted to hear. They would go out where he was to hear John and be baptized into this repentance.

The Jewish leaders in Jerusalem kept an eye out for troublemakers who distorted their laws and led the people astray. They decided to send a group up north from Jerusalem to check on this man and what he preached. Nicodemus went with them. He was curious about what was being said about John. There had been movements of this kind over the years. They would cause a stir and before long die out. Maybe this was one of those, maybe it wasn't.

When they arrived they met with the man. They asked him what his business was there. His response was, "I baptize with water for repentance. But after me will come one who is more powerful than I, whose sandals I am not fit to carry. He will baptize you with the Holy Spirit and with fire." Something about that statement struck Nicodemus' heart. Quietly, he had longed to hear something like that. He decided to stay around for a few days to watch and listen to this man John.

Nicodemus stayed just close enough to hear the man speak and to be able to see what he did. He was an investigator, and he needed information to process. The next day he noticed that John began to get excited. There was a man walking toward him, and John was pointing to this man. As the man neared he could hear John say, "Look the Lamb of God, who takes away the sins of the world! This is the one I meant when I said, 'A man who comes after me has surpassed me because he was before me'." Nicodemus was well versed in the Scriptures about the promised One, but he wondered, "Could this man be the fulfillment of that promise?" He was so plain, so ordinary. He did not have the look of the educated, refined leaders of Jerusalem. To Nicodemus, he certainly did not look like a promised king.

Nicodemus made his way back to Jerusalem, where he was one of the Jewish religious leaders. As one of the experts in the Law of Moses, he was an important man. He was respected by the people of Jerusalem — maybe even feared by a few. The clothes he wore signaled he was important. The people would bow as he passed. He enjoyed being important. He could actually trace his Jewish ancestry to show that he was a true son of Abraham. He was proud of that heritage. But now that he was back, he found his mind wandering back to those few days in up north with John and his disciples.

Nicodemus heard about a man named Jesus who had come to Jerusalem. There were rumors about him. Supposedly he had a following from people in Galilee. There was talk about him having the power to heal. He had already offended some of the people of Jerusalem. He had gone into the Temple and run out all the vendors. He had called the Temple "My Father's house." Nicodemus smiled as he thought of that scene. He had a great dislike for all those traders in courtyard of the Temple. There were more strange stories about this uneducated, simple man. Nicodemus concluded that he needed more information. After all, that was what he did. He investigated, researched, debated and eventually voted with the other religious leaders on what the truth was. Ignoring his deep feelings about this man Jesus so that he could be totally objective, he decided to pursue his personal investigation.

Here he was, a respected Jewish leader, sneaking around in the dark of night. It would not be good for him to be seen with the man. He had scouted out where Jesus was staying during this visit to Jerusalem. He was in Bethany a few of miles away from the city. Nicodemus slowed as he neared the place. He could tell he had found the right spot when he noted all the people gathered around the house. They appeared to be followers of this man from the north. He asked one of the men if he might be able to speak to Jesus, then he waited as the man went into the house.

In a short time two men came out of the house. The one to whom Nicodemus had spoken pointed at him; the other man saw him and came toward him. Nicodemus took a deep breath as he realized that this was the man to whom John had pointed back up at the river.

Nicodemus, being an educated gentleman, wanted to be polite to this man. He set out the reason for his visit in his opening remarks, "Rabbi, we know you are a teacher who has come to us from God. For no one could perform the signs you are doing if God were not with him." He had done his best to acknowledge that Jesus was a teacher by calling him, "Rabbi." He had been careful to use the word "we" so Jesus would not suspect he had come for only for himself. He had even acknowledged that Jesus was from God.

Expecting some response of respect, Nicodemus was surprised by what came next. Jesus said to him, "I tell you the truth, no one can see the kingdom of God unless he is born again." Nicodemus cringed at the image that jumped into his head. How could a grown man be born again? He responded, "How can a man be born when he is old? Surely he cannot enter a second time into his mother's womb to be born!" This Jesus had proposed the impossible.

Jesus answered Nicodemus' earthly question with words from heaven. "I tell you the truth; no one can enter the kingdom of God unless he is born of water and the Spirit. Flesh gives birth to flesh, but the Spirit gives birth to spirit. You should not be surprised at my saying, 'You must be born again.' The wind blows wherever it pleases. You hear its sound, but you cannot tell where it comes from or where it is going. So it is with everyone born of the Spirit."

Again Nicodemus was stunned at what he had just heard. Was it not enough to be born a Jew, a son of Abraham? Was it not enough to know the Law of Moses and live by it? Could this new birth by the Spirit be greater than these? Even as he had these thoughts, Jesus answered. "You are Israel's teacher and you do not know of these things. I tell you the truth, we speak of what we know, and we testify to what we have seen, but still you people do not accept our testimony. I have spoken of earthly things and you do not believe; how then will you believe if I speak of heavenly things? No one has ever gone into heaven except the one who came from heaven — the Son of Man. Just as Moses lifted up the snake in the desert, so the Son of Man must be lifted up, that everyone who believes in him may have eternal life."

Nicodemus was a good Pharisee and, as such, believed in life after death. He believed that came as a result of living out the Law of Moses. Jesus had just described another way. He knew that story about the snake in the desert. He knew the implication of what Jesus had just said, supposedly about himself. Nicodemus stood quietly as Jesus explained the plan God had — to send a son, his very own Son — to come to earth for the salvation of all people. Salvation was to come no longer through the law, but through believing in God's Son.

There was a bit more conversation. Though he had come to investigate this man and ask the questions, Nicodemus had found himself to be the student. He thought he knew the answers. He realized he hadn't even known all the questions. As the discussion ended, one of those at the house offered Nicodemus a drink. He sat quietly thinking about all he had heard. Then he excused himself and headed for home. This scholar of faith had much to consider.

Nicodemus (In Depth)

The first thing we know about this man is his name. It was Nicodemus. His full name was Nicodemus ben Gorion, the brother of Joseph ben Gorion, the writer of the Wars and Antiquities of the Jews. His proper name was Boni.

He was described as a Pharisee. In the Hebrew language, Pharisee means *separatist* or *separated ones*. Pharisees were also known as the *chadism*, which means *loyal to God* or *loved of God*. This is the group that became the bitter rivals of Jesus. They became focused on keeping a limited part of the law and the laws that they added as they saw fit. The name Pharisee may also mean *specifier*. These men saw it their task to clearly specify the Law the people were required to observe. They became the guardians and keepers of the Law. They were religious law enforcers. In their observance and keeping of the Law, Pharisees also believed in the existence of spirits and angels, the resurrection and the coming of the Messiah.

Nicodemus was part of the Jewish ruling council, called the Sanhedrin. The word Sanhedrin comes from a Greek word meaning *council* or literally, *"sitting together*." It was an administrative and judicial body. They were the Jewish Supreme Court. The Great Sanhedrin consisted of seventy-one great Torah sages, who met in the "Office of Hew Stone," adjacent to the Temple in Jerusalem. On the floor of the Sanhedrin were debated the fundamental principles of the Torah; the result was established by majority vote. So, in a real sense they decided, by a simple majority vote, what was truth and law for everyone in Judea.

Nicodemus was wealthy. Some think that at the time of the John 3 story he was one of the three richest men in Jerusalem. He was said to have spent extravagant amounts of money on his daughter. Following the death of Jesus we are told by sources outside the Gospels that Nicodemus became an open follower of Jesus. Because of the persecution of Christians, Nicodemus became a poor man. Historians of that time reported that Nicodemus' daughter was seen gathering barley corn from under the horses' hoofs.

Nicodemus was a seeker. He came to see Jesus at night to avoid the reaction of his fellow members in the Sanhedrin. He came at night so his fellow leaders would not be aware of his interest in Jesus. The majority of his peers had decided Jesus had become a nuisance to their cause. They had begun to plot ways to get rid of Jesus.

Perhaps Nicodemus came with an understanding and curiosity about the promises that came from outside the Torah. He might have remembered Isaiah 2:2-3, "In the last days the mountain of the Lord's temple will be established as chief among the mountains; it will be raised above the hills, and all nations will stream to it. Many people will come and say, 'Come, let us go up to the mountain of the Lord, to the house of the God of Jacob. He will teach us his ways, so that we may walk in his paths.' The law will go out from Zion, the word of the Lord from Jerusalem."

The John 3 story of Nicodemus' visit with Jesus consists of four major parts. (1) The first part was Jesus' explanation to Nicodemus that he must be born again. (2) Next we hear Jesus' description of the work of the Spirit in the process of being born again. (3) Then Jesus spoke of the need for him to be lifted up, just as Moses lifted up the snake in the desert. (4) Finally, Jesus told of how God's great love caused him to send his only Son, through whom we can gain eternal life by believing in him.

When Nicodemus first meets Jesus he speaks a word of respect, "Rabbi." The term signifies "great and large," and was used to suggest the large compass, a great plenty of knowledge the recipient was thought to have. After this greeting of respect Nicodemus went on to utter his belief that Jesus was of God.

Jesus turned the conversation. It was as if he and Nicodemus had been having this conversation for some time. Whatever Nicodemus came for — whatever his motives — he ended up getting the truth, as if that were what he had been seeking for years. Jesus gave Nicodemus another step in his journey of faith. He told him that to see the kingdom of God, he had to be born again. As most of us humans would, Nicodemus took that as a literal and human statement. That was the only way he could understand what Jesus had told him. In his mind he could only see the image of a grown man attempting to reenter his mother's womb in order to be born again. This would have been a troubling thought for both the mother and son!

Nicodemus must have been very proud of the fact that he was a son of Abraham. Jesus explained that it was a new birth from heaven that was needed. One should not count on birthright or obtaining salvation by working hard at the rules of the law. Salvation and eternal life are not inherited or earned: they come only from God.

Jesus showed some surprise that one of Israel's teachers would not understand more. Maybe Nicodemus' focus on the Law had limited his understanding of what God wanted from his people. Jesus told Nicodemus that he, Jesus, must be lifted up like Moses lifted up the snake in the desert.

During his visit with Nicodemus, Jesus made four dramatic statements. Three of them began with, "I tell you the truth." One of them began with, "This is the verdict."

In the first teaching statement, Jesus told Nicodemus, "No one can see the kingdom of God unless he is born again." This was quite a shock to Nicodemus. He did not understand what Jesus was telling him.

In the second teaching, Jesus talked about not just seeing the kingdom of God, but entering that kingdom. He explained that flesh gives birth to only flesh, but that the Spirit gives birth to spirit. He then tried to explain the work of the Spirit. He used something Nicodemus could understand. Jesus talked about how the wind blows. We don't know where it comes from or where it is goes. That is the way the Spirit works. People born of the Spirit will work under those new rules.

Again Jesus spoke of the truth. In the third teaching, he spoke of Moses lifting up a snake in the desert to save the people. (Numbers 21:4-9) He compared that story to what would become his story. But Jesus spoke only of the Son of Man and that he would have to be lifted up the same way.

Jesus went on to explain that God loved the world so much that he had given his one and only Son. The giving of that Son was the way to eternal life. It was by believing in him that would save the world and give those who believed eternal life. Jesus explained that this Son of God was not sent into the world to condemn the world, but to save it. Believing in him keeps a person from being condemned. Not believing in him is the way of condemnation.

Finally Jesus spoke of a verdict (the fourth teaching). He explained that light had come into the world. Evil people hate the light for fear of exposure. People who come into the light gain the awareness that the things they do are done through God.

Questions

In what ways do you see the nature of God active in the story of Nicodemus' visit with Jesus?

Where do you see the nature of man at work in the story?

What seemed to disturb Nicodemus so much during this visit?

What basic truth did Jesus confront in Nicodemus?

How do you find pride at work in your lives and the lives of those around you?

Describe your understanding of being born again or from heaven.

What is your understanding of the Spirit blowing wherever it pleases?

What changes had to take place in Nicodemus following this visit for him to become a follower of Jesus?

Some Men Came Carrying

He had been a vigorous young man. Even though he was the youngest of the brothers in his family he would often win the games they played. He was more agile than his older brothers. They couldn't catch him because he was so quick. As he grew as a boy he became an apprentice to a potter. He had learned his lessons well. Over the year his skillful hands had become those of a real artist. His ability to manipulate the clay was magnificent. He had learned to use his hands to produce beautiful paintings on his work. But now life had changed.

Even though he was still young, life was beginning to change for him. He had begun to notice the changes first as he tried to do the fine lines of painting on the pottery. He just couldn't get those lines to work anymore. Then his hands began to slip as he worked on the potter's wheel. His hand would refuse to do what he told them to and ruin his work. He would have to start over again. At first his master said nothing about what he saw. But there came a time when his work had declined so much his master gave him tasks that he could do with a pair of weak hands. Then the day came when he dropped a load of clay. His hands could no longer handle the big muscle tasks. He could not even do the simple things anymore.

His condition had continued to worsen. The day came when he could not get out of bed. His family worried about him. Day by day the young man became weaker. His muscles refused to do what his mind told them to do. He found it difficult to eat. Swallowing became a chore. His family tried to give him food, but he was unable to eat now. He was about to lose the ability to drink. Hope for the young man was failing them all.

One of their neighbors came to their house to tell them about a man named Jesus, who was in town. He was teaching at Peter the fisherman's house. This Jesus was known to have healed people. He was their only hope to save the young man. They had to get him to this Jesus. The young man had become so paralyzed he was barely able to breathe.
His father said, "We've got to get him to man called Jesus." The father and his three other sons stood silently watching him on his mat. One of the brothers ran out the door. In a few minutes he was back with rope he had cut into four pieces. The four of them tied the rope to the corners of his mat. They lifted. He had lost so much weight the ropes barely cut into their hands.

The neighbor had run ahead of them to Peter's house. As they struggled to get the young man there, he came back with a bad report. The house was so full of people they would have a difficult time getting him into Jesus. The house was even surrounded outside with people listening to Jesus. The men neared the house and laid the young man down in the shade. They had to come up with a plan. He was becoming weaker before their eyes. Life was fading from him. They were becoming desperate. The neighbor had gone back to the house to see if there was another way to get the young man into the house. He had found some stairs up to the roof. The father and brothers grabbed the ropes and headed for the house. Slowly they made their way up the stairs. They were careful not to drop the young man.

For the young man the trip had been a little scary. All he could see was the sky, the clouds and his father and brothers as they carried him. He could see trees go by as the shade changed. As they went up the stairs he feared being dropped as they wobbled back and forth. He could do nothing but hope they did a good job. They put him down on the roof. He could not turn his head, but he could tell his father and brothers were tearing away the tiles on the roof. They grabbed the ends of the ropes attached to his mat. He could sense movement again, and then he knew they were lowering him into the house. The sky was disappearing and being replaced by the ceiling of a house. He knew he was being lowered, but to what he did not know. He could hear people below him. There was quite a loud reaction to this interruption. Then he found himself lying on his mat in front of a man seated in the room.

After the dust cleared, the man looked down at the figure on the mat. They just looked at each other for a moment. Then the man looked up at the four faces peering down from the hole in the roof. Looking down at the young man on the mat, the man said, "Take heart, son; your sins are forgiven." The young man could barely notice, but there was a stir in the room after the man said this to him. This man, who was the center of attention in this room, spoke to some others in the room. He could not tell to whom the man was speaking, but he seemed to know the thoughts of some of those in the room. He spoke to them about what they were thinking in their hearts. All the young man could do was lay there. As he was still in that moment he wondered how this man knew he needed forgiveness. No one else in the room knew why he needed forgiveness except him and the man who had just forgiven him.

The teacher continued to speak to those other men in the room. Then he said to the young man, "Get up, take up your mat and go home." The young man on the mat looked into the man's eyes. He began to believe he could get up and walk. He began to feel again. He could feel his back against the mat. His breathing seemed easier. He moved. All of his body responded. He sat up and looked around at the people in the room. He leaned over and tried to stand. He rose right there before them all. He looked back at his mat. He grabbed it and tucked it under his arm. He looked up at the hole in the roof at his father and brothers. They were crying and smiling at the same time. Then he walked out of the house right through all the astonished people and went home. As simple as that, he had been lowered into this room in need of healing and forgiveness. In no time at all he had been given both. He had gone from death to life in a matter of minutes. Now he could live again.

Some Men Came Carrying (In Depth)

Read Mark 2:1-12.
Additional reading of the story is in Matthew 9:1-18 and Luke 5:17-26.

The story of Mark 2:1-12 is the story of a paralyzed man in need of the healing only God could give him through Jesus. This story has several characters. There is the man known only as a paralytic on a mat. There are the men, four men, who came carrying him to Jesus. There are the Pharisees and the teachers of the law. There is a crowd. Then, there is Jesus of Nazareth. The story begins as Jesus crosses the lake to go back to what Matthew refers to as his home. In reading this we might first think of Bethlehem where Jesus was born. Or we might think of Nazareth where he spent his early years. It is neither of those towns. The people of Nazareth rejected Jesus. We are told of his experience in Nazareth in Luke 4. That is where Jesus stood up and read from the scroll containing Isaiah in which he said, "Today this Scripture is fulfilled in your hearing." The reaction of the people in Nazareth in the synagogue that day was outrage. They said, "Isn't this Joseph's son?" They knew him and would not believe he was the one who was sent to fulfill the promise of the scripture. Jesus' response was, "I tell you the truth, no prophet is accepted in his hometown." He had to find a new base from which to do his Father's work.

Jesus chose Capernaum as his new home. Capernaum was a port town. It had a Roman garrison. It was full of a mix of people from all nationalities. The area was greatly influenced by the Roman and Greek cultures. People there were open to new ideas from around their known world. The work and words of Jesus struck a cord with many of these people. They would gather to listen to him teach. There was great delight in the miracles he performed. The people of Capernaum and the surrounding area were curious and some had begun to believe in him. That is where our story finds him on this day. There is a school of thought that Jesus was teaching that day in the house of Andrew and Simon, later to become Peter.

As people of the area found out that Jesus was back and teaching they began to gather where he was. He seemed to be able to draw a crowd. Mark 2:2 tells us, "So many gathered that there was no room left, not even outside the door, and he preached the word to them." In the crowd that day were Pharisees and teachers of the law. In our language we might think of them as seminary professors. They had come to listen and take notes on what Jesus did and said. They were the keepers and refiners of the law. They saw it as their job to keep everyone in line with the Law of Moses as they interpreted it.

One of the focuses of our story is about the next group who appears on the scene of Jesus preaching in Capernaum that day. Enter four men carrying a paralytic on a mat. Matthew and Luke tell us "some men" brought a paralytic. Mark is the distinctive Scripture at this point.

He is the only one who tells us it was four men who came carrying this man to Jesus. We are not told the name of the man on the mat or the names of the men who carried him. All we know is that the man on the mat was a paralytic. We do not know why he was paralyzed.

Matthew tells the next step in the story was that the men brought the man to Jesus. Mark and Luke give a little more detail. Matthew, Mark and Luke describe the crowd being so large the men were prevented getting the man to Jesus. They go on to tell us that somehow the men made their way to the roof of the house. There they performed some act that allowed them to lower the man to Jesus. There seems to have been some remodeling of the roof for them to be able to lower the man. Mark tells us the men made an opening in the roof. Luke says they lowered him through the tiles. The result of their work was the paralyzed man on the mat lying in front of Jesus. Can you imagine the dust and debris that was flying down on that crowd? Can you imagine how any preacher you know today would react to such a situation in the middle of a sermon?

The focus of this story is usually the man lying on the mat. But the title of this study might give you a clue that Jesus saw someone else as the main characters. In Mark 2:5 we are told of his response to this situation, "When Jesus saw their (the four men) faith, he said to the paralytic, "Son, your sins are forgiven." There are so many messages in this miracle. One of them is that there are people in the world so paralyzed they are beyond the care of natural ways of being healed. They need forgiveness that comes from our Almighty God. The only one who can make these people fully whole again is Jesus.

Another message is that there are people who need help getting to Jesus. We must take up the end of their mat and be the ones who carry them to him. We may not be able to do that by ourselves. The load may be too much for us to carry alone. We are required to invite others to help us carry the one in need to Jesus. It will be our faith that carries people to Jesus and puts them in front of him. There in the presence of Jesus the people in need will find the forgiveness and healing they need. Some days this is up to us. But we have to put down what we are holding to grab an end of the mat. It is those days the words of Jesus in John 15:13 ring clear to us, "Greater love has no one than this, that he lay down his life for his friends." God sometimes calls us to lay down our lives and put them on hold so we can carry someone to Christ.

The focus of this Gospel changes after Jesus tells the man his sins are forgiven. The Pharisees and teachers of the law are outraged at what Jesus had just said. In their minds they were thinking that Jesus was blaspheming their God. In order to blaspheme, one had to claim to be God and do what only God could do. The teachers of the law were so busy with the letter of the law they did not seem to notice a man in need lying in front of Jesus. That man's need was secondary to carrying out the correctness of the law. Jesus showed that people were more important than the law. Right over the top of this paralyzed man was a conflict between the old and the new.

Mark tells us, "Immediately Jesus knew in his spirit that this was what they were thinking in their hearts." Luke and Matthew agree that Jesus knew their thoughts. Jesus said to them, "Why are you thinking these things? Which is easier: to say to the paralytic, 'Your sins are forgiven,' or to say, 'Get up, take your mat and walk'? But that you may know that the Son of Man has authority to forgive sins..." He said to the paralytic, "I tell you, get up, take your mat and go home."

The response of the man was immediate. Matthew tells us the man got up and went home. Luke says he immediately stood up in front of the crowd, took what he had been lying on and went home praising God. Mark tells us, "He got up, took his mat and walked out in full view of them all." The dynamic healing power of God was immediate and complete. He had been healed by the words of Jesus. There is no evidence of touch involved in this miracle. The Son of God renewed his spirit and his body. In Mark's version of the story he takes special care to tell us the man walked out in full view of them all. The crowd, the Pharisees and teachers of the law, Jesus and the four men who came carrying got to watch this man walk out on his own. Just minutes before he was a man who could not move. Now he was able to walk so the world could see.

The response of the crowd should not be overlooked. Mark tells us they were amazed and praised God. Matthew and Luke agree that the crowd was in awe and praised God for what they had witnessed. That seems to be one of the goals Jesus had in his life. He wanted to bring praise and honor to his Father. He wanted people to know the life and power of God. He wanted to show that his Father was the one who could renew the brokenness of body and spirit.

Questions

How do you see the nature of God expressed in this story?

In what ways does the nature of man appear in the story?

Whose faith was shown in this miracle?

What message do you get from the actions of the four men who brought the paralyzed man to Jesus?

Are there still people who respond like the Pharisees and teachers of the law?

How do you see this story acting out in today's world?

Have you ever been called to be one who brings someone to Jesus?

The Man by the Pool

This is the story of a man we will forever know as the Man by the Pool. John chose not to tell us his name. That didn't seem important to him. We do not even know what the man's infirmity was. What we get from John is the story of the man in his present condition and the healing given to him by Jesus. We find Jesus heading for Jerusalem to be part of the Feast. As he nears Jerusalem he passes by a pool. Beside the pool are all kinds of people, who are referred to as invalids. They were the blind, the lame and the paralyzed. These people were at the mercy of others. There was one there, an invalid, who had been there thirty-eight years. John tells us Jesus saw him lying there and came to know of his condition. The man had been lying beside this pool longer than Jesus had been on earth.

We know so little about this man. We do not know about his family. We do not know who brought him to the pool each day. We do not know how he cared for his basic needs. He was not only an invalid in the sense that he could not care for himself. He had become part of a group of people cast off from Jerusalem. People coming and going from Jerusalem regularly passed this way. Maybe the first time they saw the sight at the pool it was a shock to them. But after a while they became immune to the sights and needs of those around the pool. They could ignore the sights, sounds, and smells that accompanied that mass of people waiting for a miracle to change their lives. This particular man was not only an invalid — he had become in-valid to the people who passed that way. He had become a zero, a nothing to the people entering and leaving Jerusalem. Maybe even he himself had become convinced he was a nobody.

One of the things we learn about Jesus is his great love and compassion for the humans he created. It must have been difficult to pass any group of people like this one without offering the newness of life he could give. He did not want his entire ministry to be one of miracles. He wanted people to believe in him because he was the Son of God, not because he could make the lame walk again. Yet here he found himself on the way to Jerusalem to celebrate God freeing the Children of Israel from slavery.

As he was going to celebrate he saw one who needed to be freed from whatever kept him in slavery. The man he approached was not free to move of his own will. He was apart from his family. His situation was seen to be a result of sin. He was unclean in the eyes of the good Jews of that day. He was not able to go to the temple and be a part of the Feast. He had to lie by the pool and watch as the clean people made their way in to Jerusalem to worship and celebrate. He was a nothing and an invalid. But Jesus gave him importance because he experienced God in the flesh stopping to talk to him.

We can read this story over and over and maybe miss the importance of the question Jesus asked the man, "Do you want to get well?" Most of us would think the man should immediately answer, "Yes, sure I do!"

When we read the account by John, we may miss the pause between Jesus' question and the man's answer. As he lay by the pool he had to think about whether he wanted to get well or not. He had lived for nearly four decades this way. What other way could he live? What would he have to give up if he got well? He may have had some fear of giving up being the way he was now. This life wasn't great, but it was the only one he knew. If people gave up their pity for him, how would he live? Therefore, his response was not to answer the question. He laid blame for his situation on those around him. It wasn't his fault that he couldn't get into the water when the angel troubled it. He could only lie there and watch as others got healed each time. He had to stay on his mat as the newly whole person walked away from the pool.

Jesus might have stooped down to be eye to eye with the man, whom he knew had ducked the question. Rather than dealing with the excuse, he said to the man, "Get up! Pick up your mat and walk."

Slowly the man felt life come back to his body. The bones and joints became free and flexible again. His muscles had strength they had not had in years. He could feel and know something wonderful had happened to him. He did not know who it was that was telling him to walk again, but he knew this man had healed him.

The man, who had been an invalid, picked up that old mat of his and walked away from the pool. He did not look back. He did not say, "Thank you." He did not say,

"Praise God." He just walked away from the man who had changed his life. When questioned later about who had done this for him he referred to Jesus as "the man who made me well." The man by the pool had only displayed his faith in Jesus by standing and walking away from the pool. Jesus did not say, "Your faith has made you whole." But the man must have believed Jesus had the authority and power to make this thing happen. He had to learn to live life as a somebody — a somebody who could walk.

The Man by the Pool
(In Depth)

John places this story about the man by the pool in what is probably the second year of Jesus' ministry. We are rarely aware that much of what we read in the Gospels begins in his second year of preaching, teaching and healing. In the Gospel of John we have already been told of Jesus' existence before the earth was created. John the Baptist has proclaimed Jesus to be the Messiah. Jesus has turned water into wine at the wedding in Cana. He has gone to Jerusalem and cleared the Temple. Jesus has met with Nicodemus. On his way back to Galilee he met and talked with the woman at the well outside of Sychar. He has preached in Galilee. He healed the son of a government official while there.

In chapter five of the Gospel of John we find Jesus heading back to Jerusalem for the Feast of the Jews. By the time he reached the pool of in the story, he was just outside the gates of that city. The reason Jesus was going to Jerusalem was to fulfill the law requiring a good Jewish man to do so. Exodus 23:14-17 describes that every

Jewish male had to observe three festivals each year. The first was the Feast of Unleavened Bread (Passover). The second festival was the Feast of Harvest with the first fruits of the crops sown in the field, and the third was the Feast of Ingathering at the end of the year, when the crops were gathered. "Three times a year all the men are to appear before the sovereign Lord." (Exodus 23:17).

As Jesus neared Jerusalem he came toward the Sheep Gate. This was literally the gate designated for bringing sheep into Jerusalem. Why would people bring sheep to Jerusalem? There in the Temple these sheep would be sacrificed.

Jesus seemed to know that people who listened to him preach and teach knew about that gate. In John 10:7-10 Jesus called himself the gate for the sheep. The difference in him as the gate (rather than the Sheep Gate) is what happens to the sheep. Those going through the Sheep Gate at Jerusalem were sacrificed.

Five colonnades, or porches covered the pool mentioned in the story. They gave some relief from the sun for those who were lying around the pool. The people round the pool were those with infirmities — those known as invalids. The pool was also known as the "sheep pool," "calf pool" and "heifer pool." It is thought that the pool was a place for the unclean to wash. There is some indication the pool was rectangular in shape and was divided into two sections. On all four sides were colonnades, or porches, and there was a fifth colonnade that divided the pools. Some think the pool was used to wash the internal parts of the sacrifices.

John 5:3 describes for us those who were by the pool. They were the blind, the lame and the paralyzed. They were the great unclean. Lepers were the only people in worse condition than these people. The lepers could not even come near this outcast group by the pool. This group by the pool was the great forgotten of Jewish society. They thought that maybe, being by the pool, they would get some occasional handout from those going to sacrifice at the Temple. Whatever they got, it could only come as a handout from a passerby.

However, getting a handout was not the only reason they were there. There was a more important reason. This is shown to us in John 5:4. Depending on what version of the Bible you read, you may or may not have this verse in the story. This verse carries some importance because it shows up later in the answer the man gives to Jesus' question. In the King James Version that verse says, "For an angel went down at a certain season into the pool and troubled the water: whosoever then first after the troubling of the water stepped in was made whole of whatsoever diseases he had."

John now focuses on the one who catches Jesus' eye. In this crowd by the pool there was this unnamed man who has spent a lifetime lying there getting handouts and waiting for the angel to trouble the water. We know from John that Jesus made a special effort to find out this man's story. John does not tell us how many other people are there by that pool. Surely there was a considerable audience that day. We cannot know why Jesus picked this one man out of that group by the pool. We have no evidence that Jesus healed anyone else that day. Maybe he did, maybe he didn't — we just don't know. John focused on this man's story for that day at the pool. The importance of this man's healing is what John gives us.

In John 5:5 we are told Jesus asked the man a question, "Do you want to get well?" We cannot know what was going through the man's mind as he pondered the question. He had been doing life the way it was for a long time. He had to work through giving up life the way he knew it. His thought process would have been no different that day from our thought process today. We, like that man, put ourselves in a way of life that we may not want to change. We may have become invalids in some ways. We create systems that work for us, but they may be unhealthy or dysfunctional, and some may even be destructive. When asked the question, "Do you want to get well?" we may stutter and stammer a bit before we answer. Or we may take the path the man took that day by the pool.

It seems the invalid man tried to show some respect for Jesus. He did call him, "Sir." But as we read the story we may pick up a certain tone in his voice, as if he had said, "Well, Mister!" Then the invalid man began to do what a lot of us do. He began to make excuses for why his miracle of healing had not come. There was just no way for him to get well. When the angel troubled the water, there was no one there who would help get him in the pool and be healed. It wasn't his fault. He was helpless. It was always someone else's fault. He was the victim. He did not know how to live without being a victim.

Notice that Jesus did not wait for an answer. Neither did he condemn the man or put him on the defense. It was as if Jesus knew the man's deepest fears and desires. He simply said, "Get up! Pick up your mat and walk."

But there was nothing simple about that statement. It meant that if the man believed Jesus' words, his life would be totally different. A lifetime of lying on a mat around a pool would be over and he would walk into Jerusalem on his own. People would see him and maybe ask, "Aren't you the man that has lain by the pool for years?"

In all those years that man by the pool had probably never known some stranger to take such an interest in him. He had received the handouts and the looks that went with them. But this man was different. He offered a new life to him. No one had ever spoken to him with so much authority. He actually believed what the man had said. For the first time in his life he knew he could walk. This man, this stranger had given him the permission and the power to be healed.

Later we find out this man did not even know who it was who healed him. All he knew was that he had been this way for thirty-eight years and now he was whole. He still had some way to go, but at least he could walk.

When Jesus enters our lives we are sometimes confronted by the things hidden inside us that make us an invalid. They may be things so deep inside that we don't want to let them out. These things make our lives uncomfortable, maybe even miserable. But we don't want to let them go. Jesus asks us if we want to get well and we hesitate. We fear the changes that bring freedom, and along with it, responsibility. What if we suddenly find ourselves responsible for our own situation, our relationship with God and our relationships with other people? Jesus comes with compassion, power and permission for us to change. He does not force a decision on us. In his love he invites. We decide if we want to be whole. He is ready with the miracle.

Questions

How is the nature of God expressed in this story?

In what ways does the nature of man appear in the story?

What seemed to be the purpose of Jesus for this man by the pool?

Where was faith expressed in this story?

In what ways did Jesus heal the man by the pool?

Bill Nichols

The Man Possessed by Evil Spirits

As he sat on a large rock his eyes began to clear. His agitated movements stopped. He began to survey the area around him. He realized he was naked. His body was covered with cuts. He was not much more than skin and bones. He felt hands on him as he some men led him down to the nearby lake. There they had him bathe. As he bathed he noticed what seemed to be pigs floating in the lake. That seemed odd to him. The bathing was painful because of the cuts. When he had completed his bath the men gave him some clean clothes and a pair of sandals. They also gave him something to eat.

When he had finished his meal, he went back to sit on the rock. He motioned to one of the men to join him. This man asked what he wanted. The man on the rock, newly cleaned and clothed, asked the man what day it was. He heard the answer and thought about that for a moment. Then he asked what year it was. Again the answer came. The man sitting on the rock let that information sink in for a while. Then his face began to change, and a tear slowly ran down his cheek. The man with him asked if there was something wrong. The man on the rock said, "Yes, I am missing ten years of my life. Do you know what happened to me in those ten years?" The man sitting with him pointed at a man standing in the middle of a group and said, "I will let him explain this to you."

The man helping him went over to the group, pointed back to the man on the rock and said something to the man in the middle of the group. This man separated himself from the group, walked over to the rock and sat next to the man. After a time of silence the stranger said, "My name is Jesus." The man on the rock nodded at the stranger and asked, "Do you know what happened to me?" Jesus began to tell the man about his the recent events in his life.

He told the man how he, Jesus, along with his followers, had arrived on that shore. They had happened upon the site near these tombs. They heard mournful howls coming from the direction of the tombs, so Jesus had sent some men to investigate. "What they found was you," Jesus told him, "you were moving back and forth and making strange noises. You were bleeding from what appeared to be cuts all over you." The man on the rock looked up at Jesus and asked, "Did you think I was crazy?" Jesus answered, "We weren't sure what to think about you at the time." "Then what happened?" asked the man.

Jesus began to explain how he saw this man they had found, with no clothes and with matted hair, coming toward him. "You kneeled before me when you came to me," Jesus told him. Then Jesus told the man of the strange voice — not the voice of the naked man — that spoke to him in recognition. "You mean, I knew who you were?" the man said. Jesus said, "No, it wasn't you who knew me, but evil spirits in you." "Evil spirits?" the man asked. "Yes, evil spirits! You were completely possessed by evil spirits," Jesus told him. Then Jesus went on to tell the man of his encounter with the evil spirits in the man. "I asked you your name. The answer was spoken with a voice that was not yours: 'Legion, for we are many'." The man looked at Jesus in surprise and asked, "Were you afraid of me?" "No, I was not afraid of you. I saw a man in need of my help. I was not afraid of the evil spirits either," Jesus responded.

The man stared at Jesus. He asked, "How did I get here, sitting on this rock?" Jesus smiled at him and said, "That took something from me. You see, those demons knew who I was. They were afraid of me. They thought I was about to torture them. What they asked was to go into a herd of pigs that was on that hill over there. I let them do that and now you see the result floating out there in the lake." The man sitting on the rock had to take some time to absorb what he had just heard. The man looked at Jesus and said, "Did you say the demons knew you?" Jesus nodded. "What was it they called you?" the man asked. "They called me Jesus, Son of the Most High God," was the answer. The man asked, "Is that really who you are?" Jesus looked him in the eye and said, "Yes!"

There was a stir up on the ridge above the area of the tombs. It was people from the town and the nearby countryside. The keepers of the herd of pigs had run to tell everyone in the area what they had witnessed. The people had come out to see for themselves. When they arrived they became afraid. There near the tombs sat two men. They did not know one of the men, but the other they recognized. He had been the wild man who roamed in the tombs, often breaking chains that were used to confine him. There he sat, all clean and dressed and talking to the stranger. The man healed from his evil spirits looked at this crowd of his neighbors. In the crowd he saw his mother and father. Next to them were his wife, his daughter and his son. They all seemed unsure about what they saw. There was a mixture of joy and fear in their eyes.

The other people on the ridge began to yell at Jesus and those with him. They shouted, "Go away! Go away!" Jesus and his disciples gathered themselves and headed for their boat to leave the area. The man who had been healed yelled out to Jesus asking if he could go with him. Jesus told the man, "Go home to your family and tell them how much the Lord has done for you, and how he has had mercy on you."

And that is just what the man did. He went home and told his family. Then he told those in his town. And from there he went to the entire region to tell people what Jesus had done for him. And all the people were amazed.

The Man Possessed by Evil Spirits (In Depth)

The story of Jesus meeting the insane hermit is found in Matthew, Mark and Luke. Those three agree that Jesus had to sail to the east side of the Sea of Galilee to get to the region in the story. He probably sailed from northwest to southeast. His trip probably started in Capernaum. We are told he came to the region of the Gadarenes in Matthew or the region of the Gerasenes found in Mark and Luke. The area in question would have been found on the southeast part of the Sea of Galilee or, as some called it, the Sea of Tiberius. The two areas mentioned were still some distance from the lake. It is likely that the regions of the towns were considered to be part of the area where Jesus landed.

The Matthew account of this story introduces us to two men who were demon-possessed. Mark and Luke speak only of one demon-possessed man. Mark gives us more detail about the man than do Matthew and Luke. Matthew speaks of the two men coming to Jesus from the tombs. They were so violent the people of the area had just stopped going near them for any reason. Luke explains that the man had not worn clothes or lived in a house for a long time. His home was the tombs. Mark tells us the man was possessed with evil spirits, and that he had come out to meet Jesus. He had lived in the tombs for an unspecified time. Mark implies that at one time the man had been bound hand and foot, but as he became increasingly violent, no one could bind him. The evil spirits gave him great strength. His strength prevented anyone coming near and attempting to bind him. There is no wonder everyone in that area was afraid of the man. He lived in the tombs — which correspond to our local cemetery. He wore no clothes, and was so strong he was scary. On top of all that, he spent day and night screaming and cutting himself with stones.

Matthew reports that the two men cried out, "What do you want with us, Son of God? Have you come here to torture us before the appointed time?" The evil spirits dwelling in the men knew who Jesus was. The spirits, or demons, seemed to know that God has appointed a time whey they would be subject to torture for their deeds. Mark and Luke tell us that this man possessed by demons came to Jesus and fell at his feet. Even the demon had to respect who Jesus was. The man then asked Jesus what he wanted with him. Mark and Luke tell us the man called him, "Jesus, Son of the Most High God." Again, we see that the demons possessing this man recognized Jesus. The evil spirits then pleaded for Jesus not to torture him. We can only suppose this plea came in a voice that was not that of the man, but that of evil spirits in him.

We may never comprehend the grace that filled Jesus that day as he met with the man who was demon-possessed. Even in dealing with the demons Jesus displayed tremendous mercy. Jesus asked the man his name. The response from the man was, "Legion," for there were so many evil spirits in him. Opinions vary about how many men were in a Legion in the days of the Roman Empire. The numbers range from 3,000 foot soldiers and 300 cavalry to 6,666 foot soldiers and 12,500 cavalry. The response "Legion" simply tells us the great number of evil spirits that had made their home in this man. In the Luke account it is here that the evil spirits plead with Jesus not to send them into the Abyss, a place where Satan and his minions would be sent at God's appointed time.

The Gospel accounts agree on what happened next. There was a large herd of pigs nearby where Jesus and the man sat. Mark has the number of pigs to be about 2,000. At their request Jesus allowed the evil spirits to enter the pigs. The result was that the pigs ran down a steep embankment into the lake and drowned. A miracle of healing had just happened!

Those watching the miracle of healing did not respond with great joy and enthusiasm. They were frightened by this event. They hurried back into the town out to the region to tell everyone what had happened. The result of their spreading the news was that the people from the region came out to see for themselves the report of the men. These were the same people who had been afraid of the man or men living in the tombs. Mark and Luke tell us when the people arrived, they found this previously demon-possessed man dressed and in his right mind. The people became afraid. The sight of the pigs floating in the lake probably didn't help much. They were so afraid they asked Jesus to leave the area. Instead of being thrilled for the demon–possessed man, all they could do was show fear of Jesus. There before them stood the Son of God, ready to meet them and their needs. They could only be filled with fear.

After this Matthew is silent. Mark and Luke tell us that Jesus got back in the boat to leave as he had been requested. The formerly demon-possessed person asked Jesus if he could go with him. In Mark, Jesus refused the request, saying to him, "Go home to your family and tell them how much the Lord has done for you, and how he has had mercy on you." Luke tells us Jesus says to the man, "Return home and tell how much God has done for you." Then Luke tells us the man not only went home, but also to the greater area around his home, called the Decapolis. This was ten cities of the region, bound in a loose union. Although it was a good-sized area, the healed man thought it was worth his time to spread his story throughout the entire region. The people must have been amazed when they heard his story. There before them was the man who had lived in the tombs, and now he was telling them what God had done in his life.

Questions

How do you see the nature of God at work in this story?

Where do you see the nature of man at work in the story?

What did the evil spirits want from Jesus?

How do you explain that the evil spirits knew who Jesus was?

In what ways did Jesus heal the man possessed by the evil spirits?

What was the reaction of the people who came out to investigate?

How do people today react to the work of God in the lives of people?

The Rich Young Man

The young man stood in the shadows. He didn't want to be seen right at the moment. Even though he thought he was hidden those who went with him everywhere gave away the fact that he was there. Across the street sat a man surrounded by a crowd of people. It was true. Jesus was back in Capernaum. As the young man watched him, Jesus had gathered children around him. The young man strained to hear what was being said. What he heard was Jesus blessing those small children.

The young man had to quiet those standing around him so he could hear what Jesus said. As he listened he heard the last part of what Jesus said, "The kingdom of heaven belongs to such as these." Those words confused the young man. He thought the kingdom of heaven belonged to people like him. He was one of those who lived a life just a bit better than other people.

After Jesus had blessed the little children, he was on the move. Now it was time for the young man to make his move. Even though there was a large group with Jesus, the young man knew that Jesus would give him attention. The young man was dressed in clothes that would show he was a man of wealth. The group with him would let Jesus know that he was someone of importance.

The young man ran toward Jesus. He had to push his way through the followers, but that was of no importance to him. He got in front of Jesus. There he knelt down in front of him. That stopped Jesus. With his head down, the young man said, "Teacher, what good thing must I do to get eternal life?" There was a slight smile on his face, but he didn't think Jesus could see it. He had used the term, "Teacher," as he spoke to Jesus. He knew how to impress people. In calling Jesus a "Teacher" he would pretend to be one who was willing to be a follower.

Jesus responded by saying, "Why do you ask me about what is good? There is only One who is good. If you want to enter life, obey the commandments." The smile on the young man's face widened when he heard this. He was pleased that there were so many from his hometown present for this coming out of his righteousness. He was about to show all these people just who he was. If not perfect, rich and young would impress them, he was about to show them his resume.

The young man remained in his lower position even though it was just a pretense. In hearing that he should obey the commandments, he said, "Which ones?" Maybe because of who he was, he would get some special treatment when it came to the commandments. Jesus spoke slowly and clearly. He said, "Do not commit murder, do not commit adultery, do not steal, do not give false testimony, honor your father and mother, and love your neighbor as yourself."

The young man totally missed the fact that Jesus had given him commandments that only spoke to his relationship with other people. Missing were the commandments that dealt with his relationship with God. Jesus knew something about this young man. Upon hearing this list, the young man mentally checked off each one of them. He said to Jesus, "All these I have kept since I was a boy. What still do I lack?" There was a feeling of pride in him as he was able to say this in front of so many people. They needed to know that he was as near perfect as a person could be. He expected Jesus to tell him that he was perfect and there was nothing needed for him to do.

That was not what Jesus said to him. Jesus looked down at the young man and said, "If you want to be perfect, go sell your possessions and give to the poor, and you will have treasure in heaven. Then, come follow me." Things had not worked out the way this young man had thought they would. He was stunned by what he heard from Jesus. His pride changed to disbelief. "How could this be happening to him?" he thought. He had spent a lifetime arranging his life to be better than those of other people. He was young. He was rich. He had a high position. Jesus had not rewarded him with praise for who he was. He had asked him to give up the things he had accumulated and be a follower. He had to make a decision. Deep down in his heart he knew that decision had been made before he had even approached Jesus. He was looking for affirmation of how great he and his life were. What he got was an invitation to let God be God in his life instead of the idols he had made for himself. Jesus had invited him to be part of the kingdom of God. He wanted the kingdom he had created.

This encounter with Jesus had started out as a way for him to be honored. It turned out to be a challenge to his entire life. The joy he felt at first turned into sadness. He could not give up what he had worked for and achieved. The young man slowly shook his head. Then he stood. He finally looked into Jesus' eyes. What he saw was a place he would not go. He turned, looked at those who were with him and slowly walked away from Jesus. He would remember this day for a long time.

The Rich Young Man
(In Depth)

The story of the Rich Young Man begins with Jesus telling his disciples for the first time that he must die. Then Jesus heads for Jerusalem for a final visit. Along his way to Jerusalem Jesus keeps encountering people. Each time he makes a stop, people from all around bring babies and toddlers for him just so he will touch them. Some of those traveling with Jesus try to get the people to leave him alone. But Jesus turns to them and says, "Let the little children come to me, and do not hinder them, for the kingdom of heaven belongs to such as these." (Matthew 19:14) As Jesus concludes this time with the children, he begins to walk toward the outskirts of the town. At this point in the Gospels we meet a man called "the Rich Young Man" or "the Rich Young Ruler."

Not every visit with Jesus turned out with a positive result for the visitor. That is the case with this story, told by Matthew, Mark and Luke. This young man was in a hurry to see Jesus and ask him a question. The end result was not quite what he expected. It may help us to go back to the early part of Jesus' ministry — how he began and what his focus was is important to this story. We are told in Matthew 4:17, "From that time on (after his baptism) Jesus began to preach, 'Repent, for the kingdom of heaven is near'." In Mark 1:14-15 we are told, "After John was put in prison, Jesus went into Galilee, proclaiming the good new of God. 'The time has come' he said. 'The Kingdom of God is near. Repent and believe the good news'!" It will help us to know that Jesus was highly aware of a need for repentance and change in the lives of people he saw. He was bringing Good News that included repentance.

The Gospels give us clues about this man who approached Jesus with his question. Matthew 19:16 calls him a "man." Later, Matthew 19:20 and 22 refer to him as a "young man." Mark 10:13 calls him a "man." Luke adds that he is a "certain Ruler" in verses 18 and 24 of chapter 18. He would not have been a ruler in his area — he may have been a magistrate, or what is thought of as a justice of the peace. Because he asked about eternal life, we may assume him to be a Pharisee, not a Sadducee.

The way this encounter with Jesus began seems to be important. Matthew tells us that a man came to Jesus. Mark changes the picture by telling us Jesus was about to leave after blessing the children. (Mark 10:17) He was headed for Jerusalem. Mark reports that a man ran up to Jesus and fell on his knees before him. In our story this man, according to Mark, ran to Jesus and knelt before him. The kneeling was a sign of humility and obedience. This man was showing reverence to Jesus. One author suggests that the term used by Mark should be translated as "and kneeled him." That would mean more than just bending his knees to Christ. That would mean that the young man took the knees of Christ and kissed them, as customarily done with Jewish rabbis in those times. This young man was coming to the visit with Jesus with serious intent and devotion to display his obedience to Jesus. He physically displayed obedience to Jesus. His great need to stop Jesus to ask him a question was evident.

Matthew, Mark and Luke report the young man's question. In Mark and Luke, the question is the same: *"Good teacher, what must I do to inherit eternal life?"* Matthew heard it a little differently, *"Teacher, what good thing must I do to get eternal life?"* These questions help us know that this young man has been dealing with questions about a life beyond this existence. Maybe something happened in his life that caused him to consider a life after death; an eternal life. We do not know what this man thinks about Jesus. We do know that he considered Jesus a *"Teacher,"* a *"Good teacher."*

There is a lot of speculation about the motivation for the young man asking Jesus this question. We would have to go away from the Gospel and the truth it holds to come up with a reason for the visit. It is important to remain true to the Gospel story as it is written and to let the Holy Spirit speak to us about the truth of that day and the truth it holds for us today.

We need to look at what Jesus did before he responded to the young man's question. Mark reports, "Jesus looked at him and loved him." Jesus was fully with this young man in his question about eternal life. Jesus gave him his full attention. He looked at him. Jesus was busy trying to get to the next thing on his agenda, but he made himself fully available to this seeker. *Then* Mark tells us he loved him. Jesus did not view this man as a bother to his time and ministry. Jesus was full of love for the man.

As we read this story, we need to remember that when we go to Jesus with our questions he looks at us and loves us.

In Matthew, Jesus begins his response to the man's question a little differently. He says, "If you want to enter life." In Matthew we see Jesus leading the man to a life that begins now — not in the future of eternity. Matthew, Mark and Luke agree that Jesus tells the man to obey the commandments. In Matthew the young man asks, "Which ones?" Does this suggest the young man thinks the Commandments are optional? It is hard to imagine that he thought the Commandments were some kind of menu where a person could choose which ones he would obey. Then Jesus gives the young man a list of commandments to follow. Did you pay attention to the list? Did you notice in reading this story in the Gospels that Jesus only gave a list of six commandments, not the total of ten? Which ones are missing?

Jesus told the young man, "Do not murder, do not commit adultery, do not commit murder, do not steal, do not give false testimony and honor your father and mother." These are all commandments that touch man's relationship to man. The ones that are missing are the ones that deal with man's relationship with God: "You shall have not other gods before me," You shall not make for yourself an idol," You shall not misuse the name of the Lord your God" and "Remember the Sabbath day by keeping it holy."

The Gospel writers do not tell us why Jesus only gave the young man the last six commandments. We can only guess that the young man knew the commandments well enough to know which ones Jesus omitted. We are also left to speculate on why Jesus only gave the ones dealing with human relationships. As we study Jesus and his visits with people we will discover that Jesus knows a great deal about the people standing before him. This understanding of Jesus can help us as we examine this encounter.

The young man was satisfied that he could check off the list Jesus had given him. He told Jesus that he had kept all these since he was a boy. Did it even enter his mind that Jesus had left out four of the commandments? Maybe that was okay with him. He might have just been in the business of gaining spiritual merit badges so he could be convinced he had done enough to get eternal life. We are not sure who the man was trying to convince by saying he had always kept these commandments. But apparently Jesus knew the man better than he thought he did.

In his final response to the young man's quest for eternal life, Jesus gave him one more thing to do. The accounts of the story in all three Gospels are very similar. Matthew tells us that Jesus said, "If you want to be perfect." Mark and Luke say Jesus explained to the young man that he lacked one thing. They all have Jesus telling the young man to sell everything he has. Mark and Luke have Jesus saying, "and give *it* to the poor." Matthew has him saying, "and give *to* the poor." All the Gospels agree that Jesus then tells the young man, "and you will have treasures in heaven. Then, come follow me."

The three Gospels agree on this young man's reaction to what he heard from Jesus. He became sad. Mark reports a physical reaction by this man, "At this the man's face fell." They all agree that because of his great wealth the man went away. We must interpret for ourselves why the young man walked away from Jesus that day.

Questions

How do you see the nature of God at work in this story?

Where did you find the nature of man in the story?

What do you see the purpose of the rich young man to be in his visit with Jesus?

Was there faith expressed in this story?

Why do you think the young man was sad when he went away?

Why do you think Jesus only gave the young man a list of six commandments?

What will be missing in the young man's life?

How is the story of the rich young man being written in the lives of people today?

Zacchaeus

Children can be cruel. When he was a boy all the other children called him names. They called him "Shorty" and "Pee Wee." He was a small boy. He was the smallest in his class. Even the girls were taller. He hated his status. As a young boy he had vowed to get revenge on all those who had treated him in such an unkind way. He had vengeance on his mind. He just had to come up with a plan. If he couldn't beat them physically, he would find another way.

Instead of playing games with the other children, he would spend his time studying his school subjects. He was good in school. He found the more he studied, the better he did in class. He became the top of his class. He was good at all his subjects, but he discovered that he was best with numbers. He understood how numbers worked better than anyone else in his town, even as a boy. He would seek ways to use this knowledge to make himself bigger than everyone else.

This young man was a keen observer. He would take trips around his home town. This was so he could watch the people. His goal was to find the most successful people in town so he could model himself after them. As he toured, he became fascinated by the work of the tax collectors. He would sit and watch the people coming to pay their taxes. It did not escape his eye that even the richest people in town had to pay taxes. He listened to the people coming and going from the tax booth. They were unhappy on the way to the booth. They were furious on the way back. He had to chuckle. The only people happy at the tax booth were the tax collectors. He had found a way to seek his revenge.

He applied to be a tax collector. He had to take a test to see how well he could use numbers. No one ever scored higher on the test than he did. He was set. He had become a tax collector. The fact that he was despised for working with the Romans didn't seem to bother him. He had always been an outsider anyway. Things would not change for him. He took great joy in relieving people of their money in taxes owed the Roman Empire. Over the months and years he discovered there were more benefits to his work than he had at first realized. He found that there were certain fees he could collect for his work. This money he got to keep. It began to add up for him.

He came early and stayed late at the tax booth. At the end of the day his figures never needed correction. The amount was always right. Those who oversaw the work of tax collecting recognized him as a star in the tax business. He moved up to a supervisor position. It was not long after that he became one of the chief tax collectors. He was in charge of collecting taxes for a sizeable region around Jericho. This move allowed him to get a part of every tax booth in his region. He was now not only the chief tax collector; he had become one of the richest men in the whole area. Now he could become the biggest man in town.

He made a tour of his area to see what the rich people had done with their money. His next step was to purchase a piece of land near the center of Jericho. There was an old house on the land. He had it demolished. This caused some curiosity in his hometown. Slowly, on his land, a house began to appear. Old timers stepped off the foundation. They calculated that this was the biggest house they had ever seen. When it was completed, it was the largest house ever built in Jericho. It had one more room than the house that formerly held that title.

The townspeople watched as furniture from faraway places came to the house. They could tell that all this was expensive, and all of it paid with their tax money. Now Zacchaeus could enjoy his revenge. It mattered little to him that everyone in his town hated him, even his servants.

As he was watching over a tax booth one day, he heard a considerable noise from the south end of town. He could not hear what the excitement was about so he went back to his business. A man came to the booth and announced that the blind man who sat by the road had just been healed! Someone asked who had healed him. The man answered, "It was a man named Jesus. They say he is a prophet from Nazareth."

Zacchaeus had heard that name before. Attached to that name were stories of changed lives. People had been healed. People had been fed. People had even been raised from the dead. He thought this Jesus must be quite an amazing man. Maybe he would get to see him today.

He heard a crowd coming toward the center of town. Someone shouted, "He's coming! Jesus is coming!" The crowd with Jesus was a large one. Zacchaeus would have difficulty seeing this prophet. Most of the crowd was taller than he was. He got an idea — if he could run ahead of the crowd and climb a tree, he could see Jesus. And that is what he did. He found a tall tree and climbed up to a sturdy limb. There he could watch the crowd as it went under the tree. What happened next surprised everyone.

The crowd came into sight. He could tell which one was Jesus. Everyone surrounded him and paid attention to him. He was the obvious center of this large group. When Jesus neared the tree he slowed his steps. When he reached the tree, he stopped. He looked up at the despised tax collector and said, "Zacchaeus, come down immediately. I must stay at your house today."

Zacchaeus did not hesitate. He slid down that tree and led Jesus to his house. The rest of Jericho stood stunned. They could not believe this prophet would want to stay at the house of a thief. They watched as Jesus, his disciples and Zacchaeus went off to a house that had been built by their tax money!

That day the servants of Zacchaeus didn't seem unhappy. With Jesus came a group of disciples, who needed to be fed. With them was also the blind man who had been healed earlier. The servants took the man, poured him a bath and found some clothes that would fit him. The food came. There was eating and laughter. After the meal came the heat of the day, and it was time to stay inside. Life slowed down all over Jericho. Now that they were full, the group relaxed and talked. Jesus was the center of attention.

As the afternoon passed, Jesus spoke of the kingdom of God. He spoke of God's work in the lives of people. He told of the promise God had made and how he was the answer to that promise. Jesus spoke with Zacchaeus about the power of God and how that day the blind man had been healed. Zacchaeus sat quietly and listened to Jesus. Finally he stood up in front of Jesus. With his head slightly bowed he said, "Look, Lord! Here and now I give half of my possessions to the poor, and if I have cheated anybody out of anything, I will pay back four times." Jesus said to him. "Today salvation has come to this house, because this man, too, is a son of Abraham. For the Son of Man came to seek and save what was lost." All Zacchaeus could do was weep. Even his servants cried. They had witnessed the entire event, and they knew it was a miracle.

Late in the afternoon Jesus and his group prepared to leave. Zacchaeus came to kneel at the feet of Jesus. At that, Jesus put his hand on Zacchaeus' head and asked his Father to bless him as he went about the business of paying back what he had done. Jesus and his followers left the house. As they did, they hugged Zacchaeus. He had never been hugged so much in his life. After they left he got out the tax books. He had some work to do.

Luke 19:1-10. Jesus entered Jericho and was passing through. A man was there by the name of Zacchaeus; he was a chief tax collector and was wealthy. He wanted to see who Jesus was, but being a short man he could not, because of the crowd. So he ran ahead and climbed a sycamore-fig tree to see him, since Jesus was coming that way.

When Jesus reached the spot, he looked up and said to him, "Zacchaeus, come down immediately. I must stay at your house today." So he came down at once and welcomed him gladly.

All the people saw this and began to mutter, "He has gone to be the guest of a 'sinner.'"

But Zacchaeus stood up and said to the Lord, "Look, Lord! Here and now I give half of my possessions to the poor, and if I have cheated anybody out of anything, I will pay back four times the amount."

Jesus said to him, "Today salvation has come to this house, because this man, too, is a son of Abraham. For the Son of Man came to seek and to save what was lost."

**Zacchaeus
(In Depth)**

The story of Jesus meeting Zacchaeus is a simple one. It is also powerful. The account we have only appears in the Gospel of Luke. The story may take on a new meaning when we begin to see the larger setting of that day Jesus had in Jericho. We might even think of it as "Jesus' big day in Jericho."

Jericho was on Jesus' route to Jerusalem. He had told his disciples that he must go there to suffer many things at the hands of the chief priest and scribes, and that he would be crucified and raised from the dead on the third day. That is why we find Jesus passing through Jericho to get to Jerusalem. But the story takes a detour on the way.

We read in Luke 18:35-43 about Jesus' encounter with a blind man, whom he heals. That story begins, "As Jesus approached Jericho." This means that Jesus, upon nearing

Jericho, healed this man who could not see. Also, we are told of two other healings of blind men in Matthew 29:29-34 and Mark 10:46-52. Matthew tells of Jesus healing two men. Mark tells us Jesus healed a man named Bartimaeus. Both stories indicate Jesus performed these healings on the way *out* of Jericho.

Why is it important to take note of Jesus healing these three blind men? We need to understand that these stories of healing are wrapped around the story of Jesus' encounter with Zacchaeus. In one full day on his way to Jerusalem, Jesus stopped in Jericho and forever changed the lives of four men.

The story of Zacchaeus begins by telling us about Jesus passing through the town. He has already completed the healing of the first blind man on the outskirts of town. Then we are introduced to Zacchaeus. He was a tax collector. The local population didn't think well of men who were tax collectors. Tax collectors worked for the Roman occupying forces in Judea. They collected the heavy taxes required for the upkeep of the Roman Empire in all its locations. Tax collectors were known to charge more than was required so they could line their own pockets. We are told that Zacchaeus was wealthy, and his wealth was surely a result of this kind of activity. The people of Jericho may have felt they had a right to dislike Zacchaeus. He had become rich with their money and he was a traitor.

There must have been great excitement in Jericho that day. Jesus of Nazareth was coming through. No doubt many of these people had already heard of him and what he had been doing and saying around the country. If our timeline is right, many of them had just witnessed him heal a blind man. People clamored to see this man Jesus. We do not know what was in Zacchaeus' mind and soul, but he wanted to see Jesus.

Zacchaeus is described to us as a short man. We do not know just how short he was. We do know he was so short he could not see Jesus because of the crowd. His solution to this problem was to run ahead of the crowd surrounding Jesus and climb up in a sycamore-fig tree. These trees had big branches that could hold a man. Many of the people of that time and area considered these trees sacred, and they went out of their way to treat them as such. Jesus finds this outcast out on a limb of a sacred tree.

The crowd was surely surprised at what happened as Jesus traveled through the town of Jericho. He walked right to the tree where Zacchaeus was perched and stopped. It may amaze us to find that Jesus knows where his flock is and how to find them. That is what happened with Zacchaeus. When Jesus stopped under the tree, he looked up right at the man. He said, "Zacchaeus come down immediately. I must stay at your home today."

Here we must stop to discuss the name Zacchaeus. The Strongest NIV Concordance explains that the name Zacchaeus means "righteous one, pure one." In Jesus time, peoples' names had meaning, and many of the people in the crowd would be familiar with the meanings of names. As Jesus spoke the name, he was not only speaking the name, but was indicating another clear meaning. In front of this crowd in Jericho, Jesus was calling the most despised man in town, "righteous one, pure one." Jesus was inviting this man down to take him to his house. He was also inviting him to come down from where he was and to become what his God had created him to be.

Luke tells us Zacchaeus' response to Jesus' request was to come down and gladly welcome him. The crowd's response to this scene was to begin to mutter. They saw that Jesus had "gone to be the guest of a 'sinner'." There were in the crowd those who opposed Jesus. They were not there to worship or to learn from Jesus. They were there to catch him if he strayed from their interpretation of their particular religion. They may have also been offended that Jesus would rather be in the company of this "sinner" rather than with "righteous" men like them. They may have been offended that Jesus did not show them the respect they thought they deserved. Most certainly, many of the people in this crowd did not consider themselves as sinners.

Some time during the visit with Jesus, Zacchaeus changed. We might even refer to what happened as a conversion experience. Luke does not tell us much about what happened in Zacchaeus' house that day. If the blind man Jesus healed was with him, maybe Jesus brought him in the house and discussed the healing that could take place with a man's eyes and soul. All we know from Luke is Zacchaeus' final response to the visit. Zacchaeus stood up before Jesus. This was a sign of respect. He then said, "Look, Lord! Here and now I am giving half of my possessions to the poor, and if I have cheated anybody out of anything, I will pay back four times the amount." We do not know if Zacchaeus ever fulfilled this commitment. Many of the stories of Jesus' encounters are like that.

Jesus responded to Zacchaeus' declaration by saying, "Today salvation has come to this man, because this house, because this man, too, is a son of Abraham. For the Son of man came to seek and save what was lost." Jesus confirms the salvation of Zacchaeus because of his willingness to repent. Jesus reaffirms Zacchaeus' place as part of the covenant God gave Abraham. Then Jesus explained his mission. He came to seek and save what was lost.

The use of "what was lost," is interesting in this phrase. Jesus is not just interested in who is lost, but also what is lost. He wants to redeem and make whole all there is about us. We are also named, "righteous one, pure one." Jesus speaks to us now, wanting to save what has been lost to us. We may have to come down from where we are and welcome him into the place where we live.

Questions

How did you see the nature of God at work in the story of Zacchaeus' visit with Jesus?

Where do you see the nature of man at work in the story?

Where was faith expressed in this story?

What do you think caused Zacchaeus' response at the end of their visit?

In what ways would you say Zacchaeus was healed during this visit?

How might other people be affected by the change in Zacchaeus?

www.ingramcontent.com/pod-product-compliance
Lightning Source LLC
Chambersburg PA
CBHW052109070526
44584CB00017B/2402